What's So Funny?

LARRY SWARTZ • KATHY BROAD

Editorial Board
David Booth • Joan Green • Jack Booth

Ru'bicon © 2004 Rubicon Publishing Inc.
www.rubiconpublishing.com

Published by Rubicon Publishing Inc. in association with Harcourt Canada

 **Harcourt Canada**

www.harcourtcanada.com

Project Editors: Miriam Bardswich, Kim Koh
Editorial Assistant: Lori McNeelands
Art/Creative Director: Jennifer Drew-Tremblay
Designer: Jeanette Debusschere

Library and Archives Canada Cataloguing in Publication

Swartz, Larry
 What's so funny? / Larry Swartz, Kathy Broad.

(Bold print)
ISBN 1-897096-04-6

        1. Readers (Elementary) 2. Readers—Humor. I. Broad, Kathy II.
Title. III. Series: Bold print (Oakville, Ont.)

PE1117.S966 2004   428.6   C2004-905312-4

Contents

SMILES
HAPPY
CHUCKLES
GIGGLES
HA HA HA
TICKLES
JOKES
RIDDLES

LAUGHTER

IS LAUGHTER THE BEST MEDICINE?

warm up

Do you agree or disagree that "laughter is the best medicine"?

Do you feel better after you've had a good laugh? When you are not feeling well, do you think a good chuckle or belly laugh will make you feel better? Many doctors and scientists have proved that laughing can keep us healthy. It's hard to laugh when you are unhappy or angry, but this is the time you need to laugh the most!

FYI

It has been shown that laughing can help people with cancer, brain injuries, and other illnesses get better.

Read each of the following sentences about health and humour. Decide if you AGREE or DISAGREE with each statement.

1. Your muscles relax when you laugh. .... AGREE   DISAGREE

2. Laughter can fight diseases. .... AGREE   DISAGREE

3. Sometimes laughing works as well as taking a pain pill. .... AGREE   DISAGREE

4. Laughter is good exercise for your heart. .... AGREE   DISAGREE

5. Laughter helps to clear your lungs. .... AGREE   DISAGREE

6. Humour can be good for you on hard days. .... AGREE   DISAGREE

7. Some doctors use humour to heal serious illnesses. .... AGREE   DISAGREE

8. Humour is a good way to solve problems. .... AGREE   DISAGREE

If you agree with all these statements, you're right. All of these facts are true. A joke a day can keep the doctor away.

wrap up

1. Find out how many in the class AGREE or DISAGREE with the statements. Are you surprised?

2. Can you think of a time when laughter helped you or someone you know feel better? Discuss it with a small group.

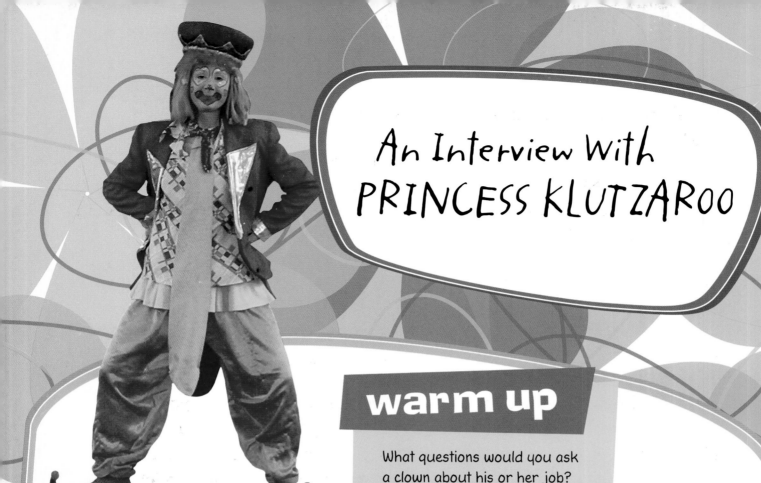

An Interview With PRINCESS KLUTZAROO

warm up

What questions would you ask a clown about his or her job?

Princess Klutzaroo got her name because she is a "klutzy" clown. Princess Klutzaroo works at children's birthday parties or special events. She has two dogs, two cats, and a large tank of fish. She went to university and studied to be an actor, a musician, and a teacher. Then she decided to be a clown. When she is not working as a clown, Princess Klutzaroo enjoys playing the piano, working as a letter carrier, and reading — and she is known as Heather Lane!

Larry: What made you want to be a clown?

Princess Klutzaroo: I always liked to perform. (Actually, I'm a bit of a ham.) One day, I was looking through the newspaper and I saw an ad for "Clown Training." That looked cool to me! I am energetic, and I love children … soooooooo … I answered the ad and became Princess Klutzaroo.

Larry: What training did you go through to be a clown?

Princess Klutzaroo: When I decided to be a clown, I took four classes that prepared me for the job:

1. Magic
2. Balloon sculptures
3. Face painting
4. Becoming a clown character (this included learning about costumes and make up)

energetic: *lively*

Larry: What is the most fun part of your job?

Princess Klutzaroo: I love to play and be silly. I am a child at heart so my job is always fun for me.

Larry: What is the hardest part of your job?

Princess Klutzaroo: I have to travel to many different places to do my job. Getting stuck in traffic is not fun. Sometimes it gets very hot wearing a wig in the sun.

Larry: What are some interesting things that have happened to you in your job?

Princess Klutzaroo: As a clown, I get to meet interesting people. I had my picture taken with Wendel Clark from the Toronto Maple Leafs.

Larry: Do you have any funny stories about being a clown?

Princess Klutzaroo: When I first became a clown, I wore white face makeup. I also wore white gloves. At one of the first parties I worked at, I took off my gloves to begin my act. A little girl jumped up, pointed at me, and shouted, "Look! It's a man! It's a man!" I was so surprised that I tripped (for real), fell backwards, and my wig went flying from my head!

Larry: What makes you laugh?

Princess Klutzaroo: It doesn't take much to make me laugh. People laughing make me laugh. Jokes make me laugh. Surprises make me laugh. The things that come out of children's mouths make me laugh. A LOT!

Larry: What advice would you give to someone who wants to be a clown?

Princess Klutzaroo: If you like to make people laugh at your jokes, a magic trick, or a clumsy fall, then being a clown might be the job for you. The real reward of the job is hearing the laughter.

Larry: Do you have any favourite jokes or riddles?

Princess Klutzaroo: Sure, I've got a joke (about a clown, of course).

Why don't bears eat clowns? Because they taste funny! *Get it*?

wrap up

1. List five interesting things you know about Princess Klutzaroo. Compare your list with a friend's. What items can you borrow from your friend to add to your list?

2. You want to hire a clown for a birthday party. List the things you might want this clown to do.

More Fun than a Bag of Marshmallows

Johnny Mutton couldn't wait for the first day he would ever go to school. When he walked into the classroom, all the kids immediately noticed he was different.

WHAT'S WITH THE NEW KID?

HE SEEMS A BIT OFF.

BUT WHY?

KOOKY, AIN'T HE?

JUST DOES.

The students each brought their teacher, Mr. Slopdish, an apple.

THANK YOU ALL.

But Mr. Slopdish was pleased.

I HAVE THESE FAKE TEETH, AND THEY'RE NOT GOOD FOR EATING APPLES.

I SEE.

OF COURSE, THEY'RE JUST RIGHT FOR EATING MARSHMALLOWS.

OH MY.

And then Mr. Slopdish said...

BEING DIFFERENT IS VERY NICE, ESPECIALLY WHERE MARSHMALLOWS ARE INVOLVED.

;GULP;

But Johnny didn't hear that because he was in the closet, hiding from those creepy fake teeth.

POOFY MARSHMALLOWS EXTRA POOFY

wrap up

Imagine you are Johnny. Write an email to a friend telling him/her what happened when you brought marshmallows for the teacher.

MISS LUCY HAD A BABY

warm up

What silly songs do you like to sing on the bus, at camp, in the shower, or with your friends and family?

Miss Lucy had a baby,
She named him Tiny Tim.
She put him in the bathtub,
To see if he could swim.

He drank up all the water,
He ate up all the soap.
He tried to eat the bathtub,
But it wouldn't fit down his throat.

Miss Lucy called the doctor,
The doctor called the nurse.
The nurse called the lady
With the alligator purse.

In walked the doctor.
In walked the nurse.
In walked the lady
With the alligator purse.

"Measles," said the doctor.
"Mumps," said the nurse.
"Nothing," said the lady
With the alligator purse.

Miss Lucy kicked the doctor.
Miss Lucy kicked the nurse.
Miss Lucy paid the lady
With the alligator purse.

wrap up

1. Work with four friends to perform this song. Each person can sing or say one line of each verse in turn. Repeat the activity, changing parts.

2. Write out the words to a silly song that you know. Make it look like a poem. What cartoon drawings can you add to this song?

WEB CONNECTIONS

Using the Internet, search for more silly songs to sing as a class.

How many times can you say "six sick sheep" without any mistakes? Why is it so difficult to say?

TONGUE TWISTERS

A tongue twister repeats one sound over and over again. This sound is usually found at the beginning of each word. For example, "six sick sheep" repeats the 's' sound.

AN ALPHABET LIST OF TONGUE TWISTERS

Alice asks for Al's axes.

Black bug's blood

Crisp crust crackles

Ducks dunk doughnuts.

Elegant elephants

Free the fruit flies!

Greek grapes

Hurry, Harry, Hurry!

Ike ships ice chips.

Judge Joe judges justly.

Knapsack straps snap.

Mummies munch mush.

Nineteen nice knights

Plain bun, plum bun

Olly oils oily autos.

Quick kiss her, kiss her quicker.

Rex wrecks wet rocks.

Short swords shine.

Ted sent Stan ten tents.

Unique New York

Valuable valley views

Which wristwatch is a Swiss wristwatch?

X-ray checks clear chests.

Yellow leather, red leather

Zelda's zipper slipped.

Girl with tongue out–Corbis; all other images–istockphoto

20

CAN YOU ANSWER THESE TONGUE TWISTER QUESTIONS?

Will wet leather weather better?
Does this shop stock cheap checkers?
When does Sherry's shortcake shop shut?
Should shy sheep sleep in a shed?
If he slipped, should she slip?
Is she a sloppy shortstop?
Which witch watched which watch?
Was the spider beside her or inside her?
How much dew could a dew drop, if a dewdrop could drop dew?

I had an old saw,
So I bought a new saw.
I took the handle off the old saw
And put it on the new saw.
Of all the saws I ever saw,
I never saw a saw that sawed
the way that new saw sawed.

Of all the smells I ever smelt,
I never smelt a smell that smelt
Like that smell I smelt smelled.

CHECKPOINT

Practise these tongue twisters in groups of two or three. Work with some friends to read the twister together, as an echo, or by dividing words or lines among members of the group.

If a good cook could cook cakes so fine,
And a good cook could cook cakes all the time,
How many cakes could a good cook cook
If a good cook could cook cakes?

wrap up

1. Clap the syllable beats for two short tongue twisters from the alphabet list. Then challenge a friend to guess which tongue twister you are clapping.

2. Try to create a sentence with a tongue twister using the beginning sound of your name. For example, Loveable Larry lounges lazily in London while licking lemon lollipops with Lulu.

How the HEDGEHOG BEAT the OSTRICH

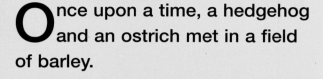

warm up

In what kind of contest or game might a hedgehog "beat" an ostrich?

Once upon a time, a hedgehog and an ostrich met in a field of barley.

"It must be very hard," said Ostrich, "when you're only as high as a stalk of barley!"

Hedgehog thought that wasn't a very polite remark. "I'm small," he said. "You're quite right about that. But I can run faster than anyone around here."

Ostrich could hardly believe his ears. "Faster than anyone around here!" he cried. "My dear, small, prickly friend! I am one of the fastest creatures in the whole world! Just look at my legs." He smiled down at those long, strong legs of his. "They are perhaps the best legs ever, for running," he said.

"I see," said Hedgehog. That's what you think. Well, what about this? Suppose we see who's quickest at running through the rows of barley in this field?"

barley: *type of grain*

"My goodness," said Ostrich. "I'm afraid there's no doubt who would come out the winner!" He ran a few yards just to show Hedgehog how fast he could run. "See? Champion Runner!" he said.

"But you will race against me?" asked Hedgehog.

"My dear friend, of course," said Ostrich.

So Ostrich and Hedgehog agreed to run against each other the next day. Meanwhile, they went around to their friends, inviting them to watch the race.

Early the next day, Ostrich and Hedgehog met at the barley field. Ostrich looked very confident. Hedgehog looked very serious. Ostrich's friends were standing around the field, ready to cheer him on. There was no sign of Hedgehog's friends.

"Well," thought Ostrich, with a little smile on his face, "they are too tiny to be seen over the top of the barley. Funny little fellows, hedgehogs!"

Ostrich and Hedgehog stood together. "Ready, set, go!" shouted one of Ostrich's friends. Off they went. Hedgehog disappeared at once, hidden by the stalks of barley.

Ostrich took great steps across the field. "One — two — three — four — five," he smiled as he left one row of barley after another behind him.

Ostrich stopped smiling. His great legs flew across the field. "Fourteen — fifteen — sixteen," he yelled.

There were twenty-one rows of barley in that field. "Twenty-one!" cried Ostrich, and his friends rushed up to congratulate him.

But there was Hedgehog. He was sitting quietly on a hill at the end of the field. It was clear he'd got there first. Hedgehog had won!

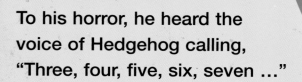

To his horror, he heard the voice of Hedgehog calling, "Three, four, five, six, seven ..."

Ostrich couldn't believe it! He began to speed up. "Six — seven — eight — nine — ten," he shouted.

"Nine, ten, eleven, twelve, thirteen ..." came Hedgehog's voice, in front of him!

Ostrich was very upset. He couldn't understand it. In all the excitement he had never once asked himself where all Hedgehog's friends had been while the race was going on.

It never struck him that only hedgehogs can really tell one hedgehog from another.

wrap up

1. Imagine you and your friends are the judges for this contest. In small groups, discuss whether Hedgehog "beat" Ostrich. You must give reasons for your answer.

2. Create a drawing to show the trick in the story.

GARFIELD

warm up

Do we read comic strips differently from the way we read other things? What's your favourite comic strip?

FYI

The Garfield comic strip reaches more than 263 million people worldwide. That is more than any other comic-strip. – Garfield.com

Garfield is published in over 2,600 newspapers worldwide.

The comic strip was first published in 1978.

wrap up

1. Do you think this comic strip is funny? Is it the words or the pictures that make you laugh?

2. Have a comic strip festival in your classroom. Bring some of your favourite comic strips from newspapers and comic collections. In groups, decide which strips are the funniest. Create a bulletin board display of the cartoons.

OUT OF ORDER

The panels of this comic strip are all mixed up.
Can you put the pictures in order so that they tell a story?

A

B

C

D

E

F

For answers see page 48.

Puzzle and illustration—Robert Leighton

Snoopy's Cry for Help

By Diane Blakney

warm up

What funny stories do you know about pets that you or others have owned?

One day, someone found a baby crow that had been hurt. He took the baby crow to an animal rescuer. The rescuer nursed the crow back to health. Then she took him out and set him free.

But the crow wouldn't fly away. For the next 24 years, the crow — now named "Snoopy" — lived with the rescuer and her family.

During this time, Snoopy learned to say a few words. People walking by the house would say "hello," and Snoopy would say "hello" to them.

In the summer, Snoopy was placed in a large cage on the front porch.

When Snoopy wanted his favourite treats (spaghetti and cheese doodles) he would lie on the bottom of his cage, with his feet in the air and scream, "HELP"!

One summer day, a police car was driving by. The police officers heard what sounded like a woman screaming for help. They jumped out of their car and ran to the house.

Imagine the owner's surprise as she walked out the door to give Snoopy his treats — and found two police officers looking at the bottom of Snoopy's cage as he screamed, "HELP! HELP! HELP!"

wrap up

1. Are there parts of this story that you find hard to believe? What makes this story funny?

2. Imagine that Snoopy was your pet. Write a letter to a friend and retell the story about Snoopy and the police. What details could you add or change to this story to make it seem like your own?

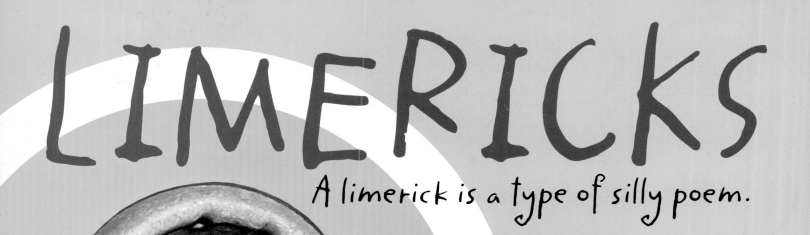

LIMERICKS

A limerick is a type of silly poem.

warm up

What rules do you know for writing poetry?

In order for a poem to be called a limerick, it must follow certain rules:

1. It must be funny or silly.
2. It must have five lines.
3. The first, second, and last lines rhyme.
4. The third and fourth lines rhyme.
5. It has a special kind of beat or rhythm.

There was a young man from Bengal,
Who went to a fancy-dress ball.
He went, just for fun,
Dressed up as a bun,
And a dog ate him up in the hall.

There was an old man from Peru,
Who dreamt he was eating his shoe.
He woke in the night
In a terrible fright,
And found it was perfectly true.

A flea and a fly in a flue
Were caught, so what could they do?
Said the fly, "Let us flee."
"Let us fly," said the flea.
So they flew through a flaw in the flue.

warm up

1. Choose one of these limericks and create a five-page picture book. Each line can be drawn on a separate page.

2. Following the rules for a limerick, write a silly poem using your name, a place you like, or a favourite animal.

Mr. Backward

Mr. Backward lives in town.
He never wakes up, he always wakes down.
He eats dessert before his meal.
His plastic plants and flowers are real.

He takes a bath inside his sink
And cleans his clothes with purple ink.
He wears his earmuffs on his nose
And a woollen scarf around his toes.

He loves his gloves worn inside out.
He combs his hair with sauerkraut.
His black dog, Spot, is coloured green.
His grandmamma is seventeen.

He rakes the leaves still on the trees.
And bakes a cake with antifreeze.
He goes to sleep beneath his bed
While wearing slippers on his head.

wrap up

1. List five funny things you learned about Mr. Backward. Beside each point explain what makes it funny.

2. Play a game with a group of friends. Each person has to describe what Mrs. Backward might be like. For example; what does she look like? What does she do? What does she wear? What does she say?

20 WEIRD LAWS

warm up

What is a law? Why do countries have laws?

MUST HAVE A LICENCE TO WATCH

Australia
- In Australia, it is illegal to walk the streets wearing black clothes, felt shoes, and black shoe polish on your face.

Canada
- In Toronto, you are not allowed to drag a dead horse down Yonge Street on a Sunday.
- The city of Guelph is a "no-pee zone."

England
- If you want to use a television in England you will have to apply for a licence.

licence: *written permission to own something*

France
- Between the hours of 8 AM and 8 PM, 70 percent of the music played on the radio must be by French composers.

Singapore

- You are fined if you don't flush a public toilet after using it.

Thailand

- It is illegal to leave your house if you are not wearing underwear.
- If you are caught throwing chewed bubblegum on the sidewalk, you can be fined $600. You can be sent to jail if you don't pay the fine.

United States

- In Oklahoma, dogs must have a permit signed by the mayor if they are to come together in groups of three or more on private property.
- In New York, a person may not keep an ice cream cone in his/her pocket on Sundays.

permit: *written permission*

wrap up

1. Work with some friends to invent three new "weird laws" for your country.

2. Create a picture that shows someone breaking one of these weird laws. Your class can put the pictures into a group book called *Weird Laws*.

Oops! I forgot the permit!

Well then, I guess I'll be leaving!

A WALK IN THE MUD

warm up

What are some funny story characters you have heard or read about?

Once upon a time, a little boy and a little girl went for a walk. It had just been pouring with rain and there was mud everywhere. The path where the little boy and the little girl were walking was muddy, too. Suddenly, the little girl's feet slid out from under her and — oops! — she fell smack into the mud on her little bottom.

The little boy felt sorry for the little girl. He caught hold of her with both his hands and began to pull her to her feet. As he was pulling her, his feet suddenly slid under him and — oops! — he fell smack into the middle of the mud on his little bottom.

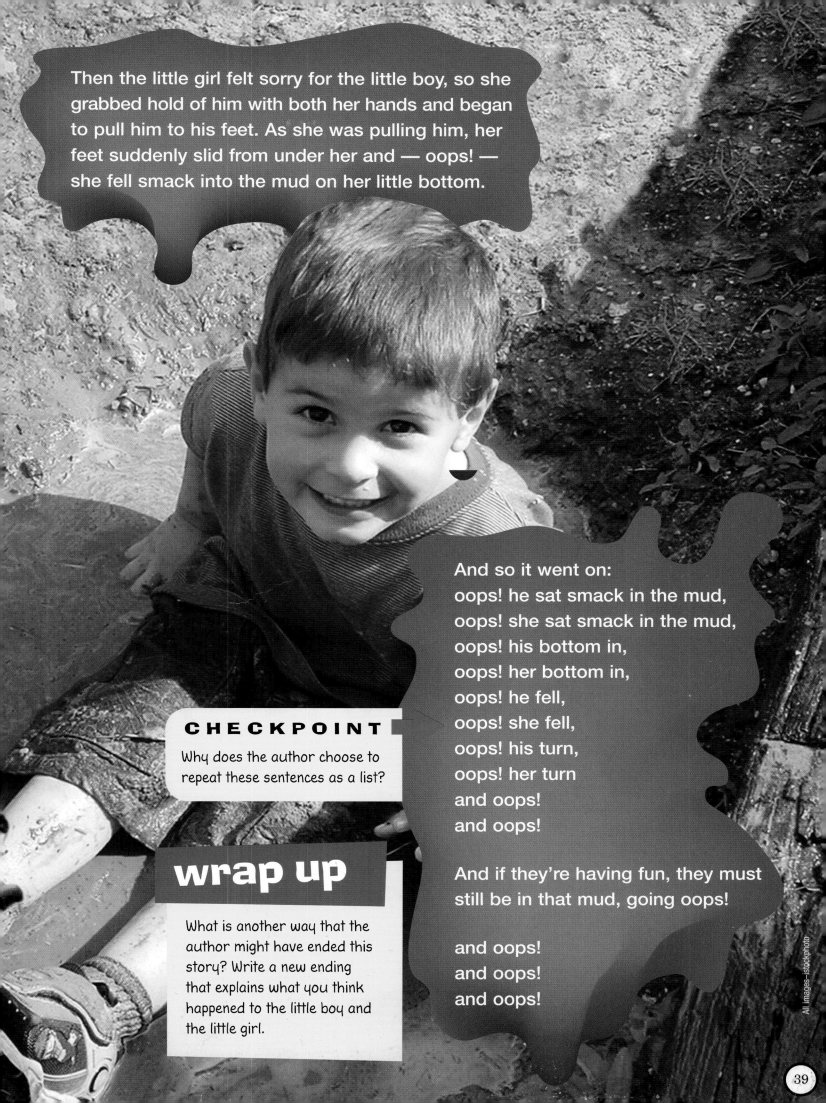

Then the little girl felt sorry for the little boy, so she grabbed hold of him with both her hands and began to pull him to his feet. As she was pulling him, her feet suddenly slid from under her and — oops! — she fell smack into the mud on her little bottom.

And so it went on:
oops! he sat smack in the mud,
oops! she sat smack in the mud,
oops! his bottom in,
oops! her bottom in,
oops! he fell,
oops! she fell,
oops! his turn,
oops! her turn
and oops!
and oops!

And if they're having fun, they must still be in that mud, going oops!

and oops!
and oops!
and oops!

CHECKPOINT

Why does the author choose to repeat these sentences as a list?

wrap up

What is another way that the author might have ended this story? Write a new ending that explains what you think happened to the little boy and the little girl.

BELIEVE IT or NoT

warm up

What is the most amazing thing that has happened to you or someone you know? Discuss with a small group.

40

Hickory-Dickory Dock

After 82-year-old Frederic Green was declared dead, he came back to life when a camera flashbulb went off! A woman from England made sure that wouldn't happen to her. In her will, she asked for her body to be checked for signs of life — so her doctor had her body placed inside an empty grandfather clock for easy viewing.

All Bottled Up

When a person died in 19th Century Borneo, the body was squeezed into a jar. The jar was kept in the house of a relative for one year before it was buried.

Borneo: *an island in the Pacific Ocean*

Handy Victory

In 1015, Heremon O'Neil was in a boating race. The first man to touch soil would rule Ireland. O'Neil won by cutting off his hand and throwing it on to shore.

wrap up

1. Do you find the stories on this page hard to believe? Explain.

2. What makes these stories funny? Draw a picture of your favourite story.

GIACCO AND HIS BEAN

By Florence Botsford

warm up

Imagine a kingdom where no one is allowed to laugh. Why might this happen? How might this change?

Once upon a time, there was a little boy named Giacco who had no father or mother. The only food he had was a cup of beans. Each day, he ate a bean, until finally he only had one left. So he put this bean into his pocket and walked until night. He saw a little house under a mulberry tree. Giacco knocked at the door. An old man came out and asked what he wanted.

"I have no father or mother," said Giacco. "And I have no food except this one bean."

"Poor boy," said the kind old man. He gave Giacco four mulberries to eat and let him sleep by the fire. During the night, the bean rolled out of Giacco's pocket, and the cat ate it up. When he awoke, he cried, "Kind old man, your cat has eaten my bean. What shall I do?"

"You may take the cat," said the kind old man. "I do not want to keep such a mean animal."

So Giacco took the cat and walked all day until he came to a little house under a walnut tree. He knocked at the door. An old man came out and asked what he wanted.

"I have no father or mother," said Giacco. "And I have only this cat that ate the bean."

"Too bad," said the kind old man. He gave Giacco three walnuts to eat and let him sleep in the dog kennel.

During the night, the dog ate up the cat, and when Giacco awoke, he cried, "Kind old man, your dog has eaten my cat!"

"You may take the dog," said the kind old man. "I do not wish to keep such a mean brute."

CHECKPOINT

How does this illustration match the story? Do you learn any new information from this picture?

So Giacco took the dog and walked all day until he came to a little house under a fig tree. He knocked at the door. An old man came up and asked what he wanted.

"I have no father or mother," said Giacco. "I have only this dog that ate the cat that ate the bean."

"How very sad!" said the kind old man, and he gave Giacco two figs to eat, and let him sleep in the pig sty.

That night, the pig ate up the dog, and when Giacco awoke he cried, "Kind old man, your pig has eaten up my dog!"

"You may take the pig," said the kind old man. "I do not care to keep such a disgusting creature."

kennel: *a dog house*
brute: *a creature that is unfriendly, violent*

So Giacco took the pig and walked all day until he came to a little house under a chestnut tree. He knocked at the door. An old man came out and asked what he wanted.

"I have no father or mother and only this pig that ate the dog that ate the cat that ate the bean," said Giacco.

"How pitiful!" said the kind old man, and gave Giacco one chestnut to eat, and let him sleep in the stable. During the night, the horse ate up the pig, and when Giacco awoke he cried, "Kind old man, your horse has eaten up my pig!"

"You may take the horse," said the kind old man. "I do not want to keep such a worthless beast." So Giacco rode away on the horse.

pitiful: *sad*
worthless: *useless*

CHECKPOINT

Can you predict what will happen next?

He rode all day until he came to a castle. He knocked at the gate, and a voice cried, "Who is there?"

"It is Giacco. I have no father or mother, and I have only this horse that ate the pig that ate the dog that ate the cat that ate the bean."

"Ha! Ha! Ha!" laughed the soldier. "I will tell the King."

"Ha! Ha! Ho! Ho!" laughed the King. "Whoever heard of a bean that ate the cat that ate the dog that ate the pig that ate the horse!"

"Excuse me, Your Majesty, it is the other way around," said Giacco. "It was the horse that ate the pig that ate the dog that ate the cat that ate the bean."

BURP

"Ha! Ha! Ho! Ho!" laughed the King. "My mistake! Of course, it was the bean that ate the horse; no, I mean the horse that ate the bean; no, I mean – Ha! Ha! Ho! Ho!" laughed the king, and the knights began to laugh, and the ladies began to laugh, and the maids began to laugh, and the cooks began to laugh, and the bells began to ring, and the birds began to sing, and all the people in the kingdom laughed and sang, and the King came to the gate and said:

"Giacco, if you will tell me everyday about the bean that ate the horse; I mean the horse that ate the bean; no, I mean the horse that ate the pig that ate the dog that ate the cat that ate the bean — Ha! Ha! Ho! Ho! Ho! Ho! Ho! — you shall sit on the throne beside me."

So Giacco put on a golden crown and sat upon the throne, and every day he told about the horse that ate the pig that ate the dog that ate the cat that ate the bean, and everybody laughed and sang and lived happily ever after.

wrap up

Sit in a circle to retell the story. Each person can tell one or two sentences. Add your own details to make the story even funnier.

PUNCH LINE

TEACHER: What do you want to be when you grow up?

GUS: Taller.

Knock Knock!
Who's there?
Police.
Police who?

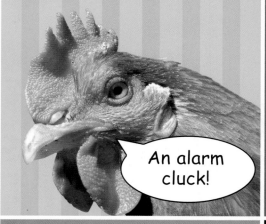

Police let me in, it's cold out here!

TEACHER: Gus, name five things that contain milk.

GUS: Cheese, butter, cream, and two cows.

Knock knock!
Who's there?
Europe.
Europe who?
Europe early today.

What do you get if you cross a wake-up call with a chicken?

An alarm cluck!

Knock Knock!
Who's there?
Doris.
Doris, who?
Doris locked, that's why I had to knock!

FYI

Comedian Wee Georgie Wood is said to have told the first knock-knock joke on a radio program on 14 November 1936.

CHECKPOINT

Do you "get" the punch lines? Did they make you laugh?

TEACHER: Gus, spell mouse.

GUS: m-o-u-s

TEACHER: That's almost right. What's at the end?

GUS: A tail.

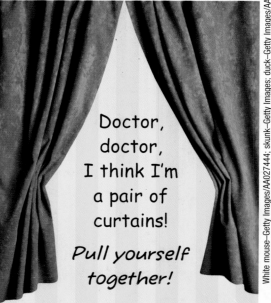

Doctor, doctor, I think I'm a pair of curtains!

Pull yourself together!

46

HA! HA! HA! HE! HE! HE!

Two muffins are baking in an oven. One says to the other:

Hot in here, isn't it?

And the other one screams:

AHHHH! A talking muffin.

Doctor, doctor, I think I'm shrinking!

You'll just have to be a little patient.

Knock Knock!
Who's there?
Norma Lee.
Norma Lee who?
Normalee I don't go around knocking on doors, but do you want to buy a set of encyclopedias?

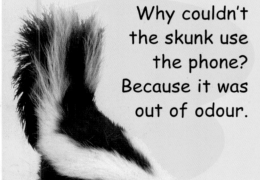

Why couldn't the skunk use the phone? Because it was out of odour.

A duck walks into a drugstore and asks for some lip balm. "Cash or charge?" asks the clerk.

Oh, just put it on my bill.

Knock knock!
Who's there?
Alaska.
Alaska who?
Alaska later.

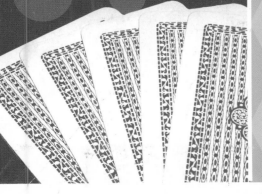

Doctor, doctor I think I'm a deck of cards!

You will just have to deal with it.

Did you hear the one about the dog who went to the flea circus?

He stole the show!

wrap up

1. Which joke or jokes made you laugh out loud? Why? Survey your friends using the same questions. Which joke is the funniest?

2. Working alone or with a partner, make a tape recording of some favourite jokes and riddles to share with others.

OUT OF ORDER Answers *(from page 27)*

ACKNOWLEDGEMENTS

The publisher gratefully acknowledges the following for permission to reprint copyrighted material in this book.

Every reasonable effort has been made to trace the owners of copyrighted material and to make due acknowledgement. Any errors or omissions drawn to our attention will be gladly rectified in future editions.

Diane Blakney: "Snoopy the Bird," www.all-creatures.org.

"Mr. Backwards" from *Bing Bang Boing*, copyright © 1994 by Douglas Florian, reprinted by permission of Harcourt, Inc.

Really, Really Bad Jokes. Text Copyright © 1999 Katy Hall. Illustrations Copyright © 1999 Rick Stromoski. Reproduced by permission of the publisher Candlewick Press, Inc., Cambridge, MA.

"Believe It or Not," From *Ripley's Believe It or Not Special Edition* by Mary Packard. Copyright © 2004 by Ripley Entertainment. Reprinted by permission of Scholastic Inc.

"More Fun than a Bag of Marshmallows" from *The Many Adventures of Johnny Mutton*, copyright © 2001 by James Proimos, reprinted by permission of Harcourt, Inc.

"Out of Order," excerpted from the book GAMES MAGAZINE JUNIOR KIDS' BIG BOOK OF GAMES © 1987, 1988, 1990 BY psc Games Limited Partnership Used by permission of Workman Publishing Co., Inc., New York All Rights Reserved

GARFIELD © 2000 Paws, Inc. Reprinted with permission of UNIVERSAL PRESS SYNDICATE. All rights reserved.